The Sun and the Moon

Emily Kington

Contents

Words that appear in **bold** are explained in the glossary

Discover more at **www.hungrytomato.com**

Sun and Moon

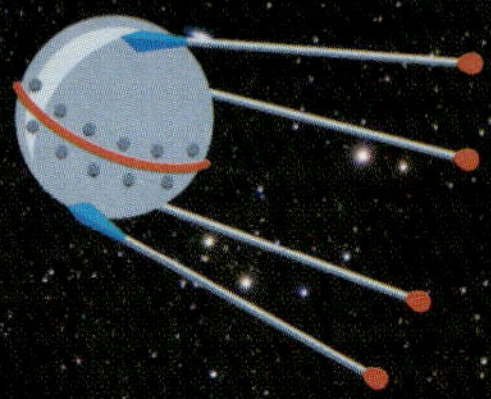

The Sun provides light and heat to our whole **solar system.** Its light helps us see other moons and planets.

Our Moon is the brightest object in our night sky.

The Moon doesn't produce light. It looks bright because it **reflects** light from the Sun.

Without the Sun our planet would be a gigantic icy rock.

Scientists think the Moon was made when an object smashed into Earth. Pieces of our planet flew off into space, stuck together and made the Moon!

How Far to the Sun?

The Sun is at the heart of our solar system. Planets and other space objects within the solar system travel around the Sun in what is called an **orbit.**

Our Earth and Moon are about 93 million miles (150 million kilometres) from the Sun.

If you were able to travel to the Sun in a Jumbo Jet, it would take you about 19 years to get there!

All of the planets stay at a set distance away from the Sun because of a pulling force called **gravity**.

Our Sun is about four and a half billion years old and it should live for at least another 5 billion years... that's very old!

The Sun

The Sun is very important to life on Earth. It provides energy to grow the plants that we need for food and **oxygen**. It also helps to keep us warm!

The Sun is sooooo hot that there is nothing we can compare it to here on Earth. Its centre can reach 15 million Celcius (27 million degrees Fahrenheit).

The Sun is a star. Stars create heat and light. You can see lots of stars in the sky, but they are all much further away.

We use sun cream to protect us from harmful rays from the Sun, that could damage our skin.

The Sun may look like fire, but it isn't. It's mostly made up of two kinds of **gas**: *hydrogen* and *helium*.

The Earth's Orbit

It takes Earth 365 days to orbit the Sun, that is one whole year! You can't feel it, but the Earth is zooming very quickly through space, even as you read this!

The Earth is speeding round the Sun at roughly 30 kilometres (18.5 miles) per second. That's incredibly fast!

In one orbit, the Earth will travel about 940 million kilometres (584 million miles). Phew!

The Earth orbits the Sun in an oval shape. This means that it is not always the same distance away from the Sun.

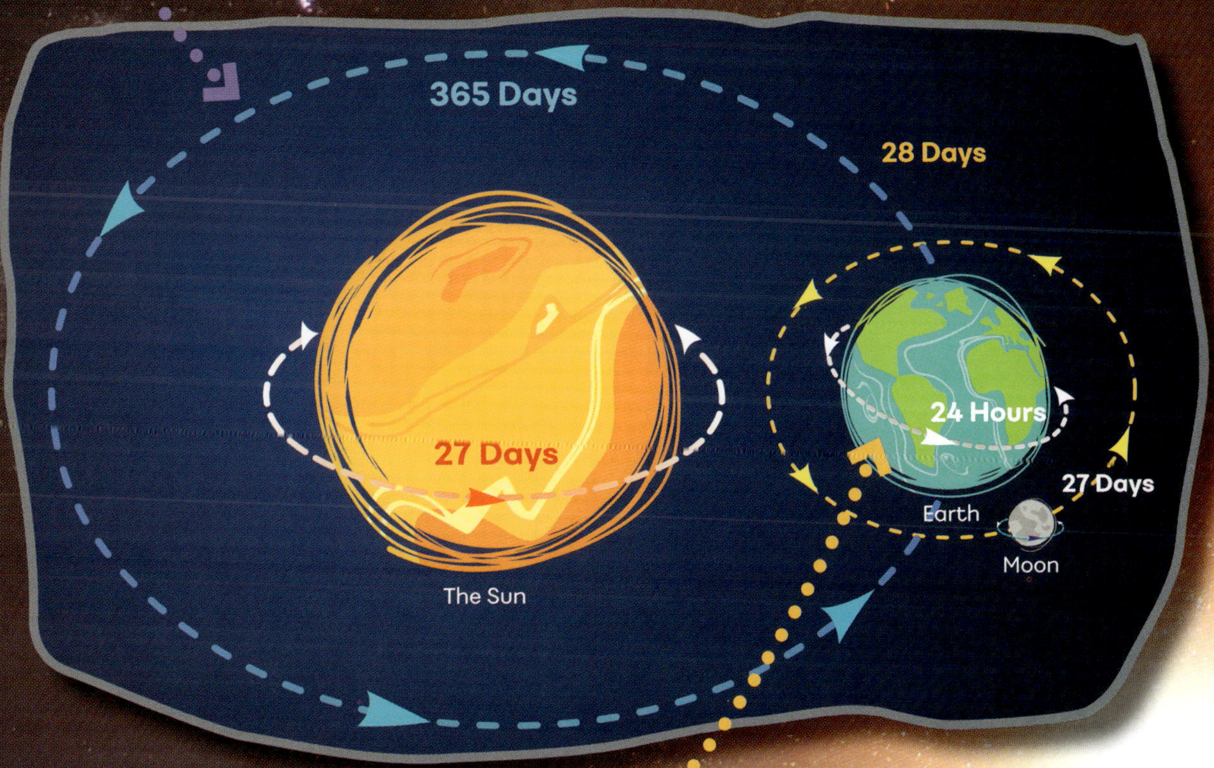

While it orbits the Sun, the Earth also spins around. It makes one full **rotation** every day.

The Moon

On 20th July 1969, *Neil Armstrong* and *Buzz Aldrin* became the first humans to set foot on the Moon, as part of the *Apollo 11* mission.

Apollo 11 was launched by a *Saturn V* rocket from *Kennedy Space Center* in Florida, USA on 16th July. It took 76 hours to enter orbit around the Moon.

We are still learning new things about the Moon. In 2020, NASA's mission SOFIA found proof that there is water on the Moon!

During their moon walk, Armstrong and Aldrin left a message that said, "We came in peace for all mankind."

The Moon's surface has mountains and lots of **craters,** and is covered in powdery soil, pebbles and rocks.

The Moon's Orbit

As Earth orbits the Sun, the Moon travels around Earth. It takes 27 days for the Moon to complete its orbit.

As it orbits, the Moon appears to be different shapes when viewed from Earth. We call these shapes the *Phases of the Moon.*

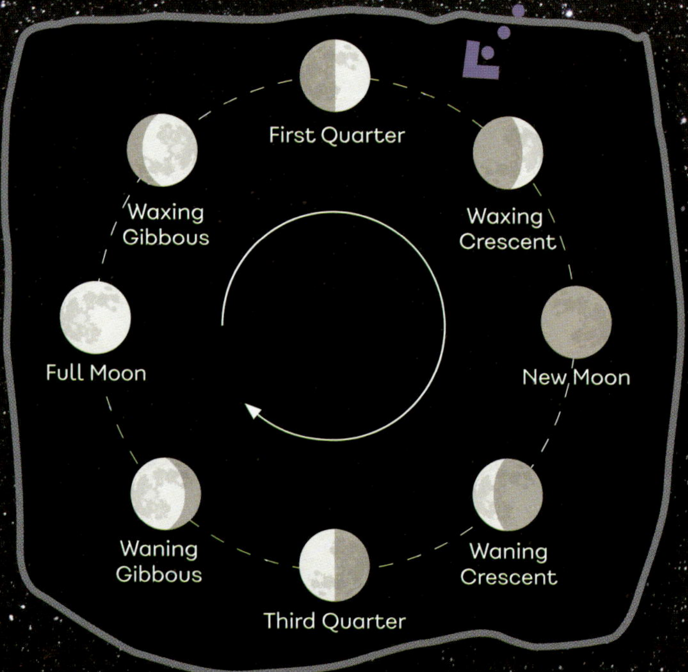

The moon has phases because the Sun lights certain areas of the Moon at different stages of its orbit. From Earth, we only see the sunlit parts.

When full sunlight hits the Moon's surface, it can make it very hot, with temperatures reaching 127 °C (260 °F).

The Moon's orbit affects the **tides** of our seas and oceans.

Daytime

As Earth rotates, the Sun shines on the half of the planet that is facing it, providing it with daylight.

The Sun appears to come up in the morning and go down at night-time, as we spin towards and away from the Sun.

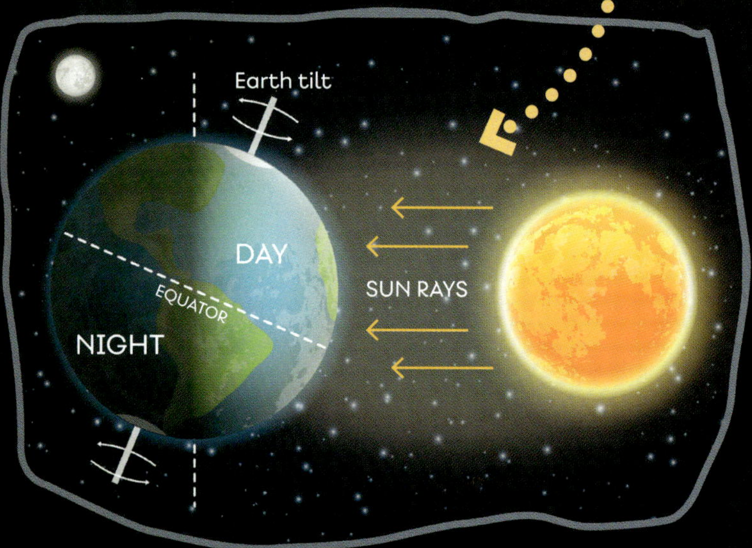

This side of the Earth is in shadow, and it is night-time.

During the day, the Sun's energy keeps our planet warm and gives us **natural light.**

Since it is night in some parts of the world while it is day in others, different places have different **times zones.**

Sometimes you can see the Moon during daytime too. This depends on its position and how much sunlight it is reflecting.

Night-time

As Earth rotates away from the Sun it starts to fall into darkness. The Moon provides some light by reflecting the Sun's rays.

Using electricity, we can make **artificial light** to help us see in the dark.

Have you noticed that it's cooler at night than it is in the daytime? This is because there are no Sun rays producing warmth.

Some night-time animals, like owls, have big eyes that pick up tiny rays of light to help them see in the dark.

In most places around the world, nights are longest in the winter and shortest in the summer.

Seasons

Most places on Earth have four seasons throughout the year. We experience changes to the light, weather and nature in each season, all because of the Sun!

Earth rotates at a tilted angle as it orbits the Sun, which means that at different times of year, the top and bottom halves of the Earth will lean a little closer or further away from the Sun.

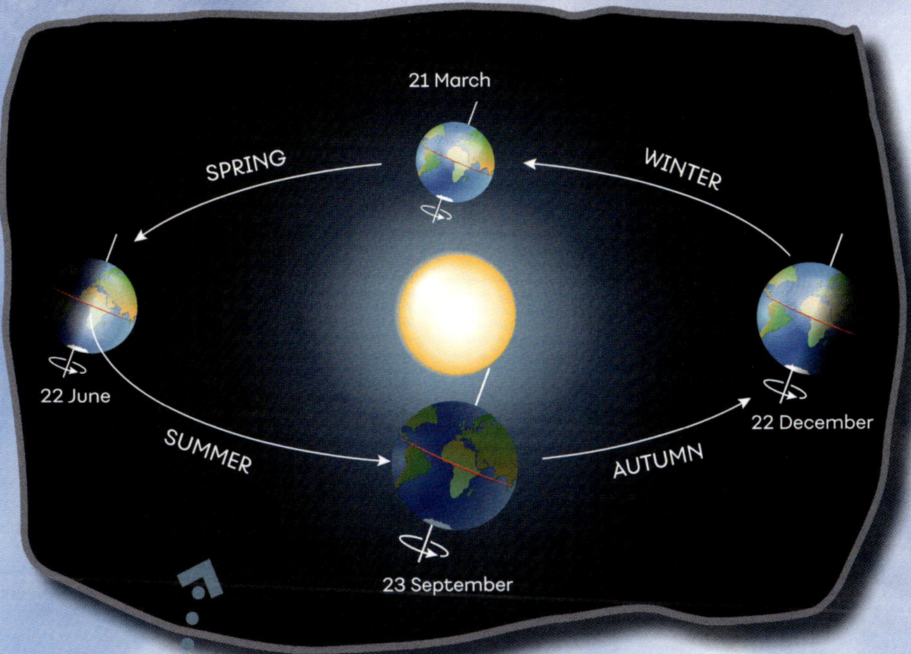

When part of the Earth is leaning fully towards the Sun, it will be summer, and when it is leaning furthest away it will be winter.

Eclipses

An eclipse occurs when an object in space, like a moon or a planet, blocks another object from view. On Earth we have Solar and Lunar eclipses.

A solar eclipse takes place when the Moon travels in front of the Sun, blocking some, or all of it, from view.

When the Sun is completely covered, we call it a *Total Eclipse*. When this happens, it gets very dark on Earth because sunlight is blocked.

A lunar eclipse happens when the Sun, Moon and Earth are positioned in a straight line, with the Earth in the middle. The Earth casts a shadow on the Moon but it remains visible.

A lunar eclipse is sometimes called a *Blood Moon*, because it makes the Moon look red.

You should never look directly at a solar eclipse. It may look dark, but the Sun's rays could still damage your eyes!

Glossary

artificial light – man-made light, usually produced using electricity.

crater – a large hole in the ground, which has been caused by something hitting it, or by an explosion.

equator – an imaginary line around the middle of Earth's surface, at an equal distance from the North and South Poles.

gas – a substance that is neither solid or liquid and has no fixed shape. Many gases are invisible.

gravity – a pulling force that works across space. It's the same force that causes an object to fall when you drop it.

natural light – light produced by the Sun.

orbit – the path taken by one object circling around another object in space.

oxygen – is a gas in the air that we need to breathe.

reflects – when light bounces off the surface of an object, it is reflected.

rotation (rotate) – when something spins around a point located at its centre.

solar system – the solar system contains all of the planets, dwarf planets, moons, and other objects that travel around the Sun.

tides – the regular change in the level of the sea on the shore.

time zones – areas of the world that are divided up according to what time they keep. Some time zones are behind or ahead of others by multiple hours.

Picture Credits
(abbreviations: t = top; b = bottom; m = middle; l = left; r = right; bg = background)

Shutterstock: Aphelleon 4bg; AZSTARMAN 23m; Baranov E 14bg; d3verro 1tr, 4tr, 6tm, 10tr, 14tr, 18t, 20tm, 22tm; Designua 21tr; diluck 11m; Dima Zel 12bg; Elena Zajchikova 20bg; Everett Collection 12ml; Feng Yu 18m; FlashMovie 16bg; Fred Mantel 23t; Gilda Villarreal 8bg; Kyle Cleary 24bg; Lijphoto 17r; Redsapphire 14bl; Rido 9br; Romolo Tavani 1bg; Romolo Tavani 22bg; Sahara Prince 4br; Siberian Art 16bl; Skorzewiak 2bg; Sunflowerr 6bg; Triff 8bm; Vadim Sadovski 10bg; VikiVector 3tm, 8tm, 12tm, 16tm, 24tr; VladKK 19tl; Yaska 20ml; Yindee (astronaut cartoons); zef art 18bg.

Every effort has been made to trace the copyright holders and we apologise in advance for any unintentional omissions. We would be pleased to insert the appropriate acknowledgement in any subsequent edition of this publication.

First published in Great Britain in 2022 by Hungry Tomato Ltd
F1, Old Bakery Studios, Blewetts Wharf, Malpas Road, Truro, Cornwall, TR1 1QH, UK

A CIP catalogue record for this book is available from the British Library

Published and Distributed in India by Scholastic India Pvt. Ltd.

ISBN 978-93-5471-942-4

This reprint edition : January 2025

Printed in India at Shree Maitrey Printech Pvt. Ltd., Noida